S E L E C T E D
L E T T E R S

✿

SELECTED LETTERS

❀

BJ SOLOY

NEW MICHIGAN PRESS

TUCSON, ARIZONA

NEW MICHIGAN PRESS

DEPT OF ENGLISH, P. O. BOX 210067

UNIVERSITY OF ARIZONA

TUCSON, AZ 85721-0067

<http://newmichiganpress.com>

Orders and queries to <nmp@thediagram.com>.

ISBN 978-1-934832-58-5. FIRST PRINTING.

Printed in the United States of America.

Design by Ander Monson.

Cover Art: BJ Soloy.

CONTENTS

Children on Television,   1

Bea Arthur, Dead at 86,   2

Antonin Scalia, Dead at 79,   3

Eric, Supposedly 32,   4

Lucia Berlin, the Average Dog Born & Dead Since
    Your Death,   5

Dearest Alice Notley,   6

Philip, Brother, Bartender,   8

Merle Haggard,   10

Our Emma, Fairest When Fleeing,   12

Oh, Torpor. My Drawl. My Poor Drawn Light,   14

Andy Williams, Dead at 84,   16

Larry Levis, Big Deal,   16

Well Hell, Birdie,   17

Khaty Xiong,   23

That Other Guy From The Eagles, Dead Not Too
    Long After Bowie,   24

Andrew Martin,   26

Robert Goulet, Dead at 73,   28

Rachel Mindell,   30

James Taylor, I Forgive You. Groveling   32

Morgan Maurath,   34

Kim Bell,   36

You, Oh You, Trying to Light a Firecracker in the
    Snow,   38

Rick Springfield, Get Off My Lawn.   39
Oh, Lioness,   40
Donald J. Trump, Hyperobject,   41
Michael Landon, Dead So Long,   43
Thomas Kinkade, Dead at 54,   45

Acknowledgments   47

CHILDREN ON TELEVISION,

You smile for me. You mean it as encouragement.
You don't mean it, but it's nonetheless encouraging

in facsimile. Thy vibrant robe a-plaid & ruffling

on our pet stink sofa-couch, don't neglect your other
addictions on account of me. I sip the tea you've made

me & the other world endures. Within this outer world
there burrows a worried other. There's no diagram.

To possess the necessary worry & to lead it up a mountain
armed, follow me, you children of the Postcard Valley!

BEA ARTHUR, DEAD AT 86,

In lieu of your head stuffed and mounted on my wall,
I have a photograph stuck in a lowly printed medium,
&, in lieu of an elegy, a story:
it ends like they all end, w/ me being swarmed
by bees, but starts in your family sedan.
I won't imagine you each of the details, but
I do miss you in a small, potent way
& regret a lot of things, though
not all that you'd think.

Tomorrow is likely a large number
of living persons' birthday, but not yours,
even were you still here. Also,
it will be a Monday, & you know what that means.
Reruns.
I don't truly believe that this building snores—
more likely its internal stirrings only make it
to my ears when all else gives it a goddamned rest.
Still, it's comforting to feel that there's
someone who, at the next loud noise, nightmare,
commercial break, will be there again.
I've decided that referring to the moon
as a recurring tumor is stupid,
& so refer to it again simply as the moon.
I haven't seen the moon for days.

ANTONIN SCALIA, DEAD AT 79,

Yesterday you were chairing my enemies list
& today you're the first Italian-American
to die in one of my poems. I write you
now this separate opinion to your Trenton
thespian explosions. We all have a West Texas
resort ranch waiting for us. We're all hunters.
Click here to comment.
I told Julie you were dead & she spit
on the floor. This is saying something,
but it was the sexiest thing she did all day.

I placed the contents of her dissent under
strict scrutiny: wine, for sure, & years
of women, queers, minorities, & retards
under your sturdy shoe. Nino, this is a love song
to your vacancy. On a long drive to a Latin Mass,
had you thought, "At least I'll leave a wake
of smoldering refuse when I finally crash this
fickle body," or did you think just about sleep?

ERIC, SUPPOSEDLY 32,

I dreamt that Dad died again & that I was in an apartment
with an ex whose brother is dead in real life. I suppose
this means I'm dreaming of death. I filled my mouth with petals

well past the point of comfort. I don't know if you have any anxiety
about age. I didn't, but I do through you. My little brother,
old. Eric, we stole your vodka & love you. You just called & I didn't

answer because it's noisy here. We now inhabit different cardinals,
different genres—you make me Western. As I ate lunch today,
a man in a well-kept beard & racist baseball hat sat alone

& ate a sandwich he was clearly in love with. I couldn't look at him
for more than three or four seconds without pre-tears swelling.
He ate slow & determined. By the time he left, I was almost empty.

LUCIA BERLIN, THE AVERAGE DOG BORN & DEAD SINCE YOUR DEATH,

She always seemed dead anyway, but nicely so,
like an illustration or advertisement.
—"Emergency Room Notebook" 1977

I enjoy my night, but feel
like I've been sold a product.
These are my strange mating displays.

Let's break bottles on each other's foreheads,
each other's doomed vessels. In turn, I am excellent
food for many predators. We frenzy for the film crew.

It's an unexpected satisfaction to see my blood
in the river's scum, as natural as the piping on your coat.
You cradle your jockey, pull out your relative's teeth, I'll
    write you

letters until you write me back. Until no pups are left for
    the whelping.

DEAREST ALICE NOTLEY,

A lot of notes lately. A snotted paper towel in my back pocket that reads, "There's always someone to fall in love w/ @ the laundromat." Does this betray a surging fear of forgetting? Or some other insecurities? A new mole. A white cloud frozen on my thumbnail. A strawberry birthmark, surfacing ribcages, wild teeth, an oft-broke nose. All as selfish, manic, continuous as chain-smoking my roommate's mail-order cigarettes while he's off at work. Also, rough drafts of letters. Lists of songs:

—Bluebird Wine
—We Dance
—Life on Mars
—Candy Says
—All and Everyone.

These among a litter of to-do lists:

—make cd
—get bike fixed
—laundry
—poem.

How long has it been since I've been naked in front of another person?

Do I leave my blinds open just so I can't answer with certainty? Just started to rain as I wrote that to you. It sounds like an air conditioner kicking in, but we don't have an air conditioner. It's rain. Unlit, after-hours rain. Strong-arming romantic rain. This is going to be about Patsy Cline now. No, I'm not strong enough to turn it. Should I have more questions for you? Do you think I'm more a cello, a singing saw, a theramin or a pedal steel? If you were to ask me (about you) my first thought was "Tuba" though I don't feel like defending it.

Does this read artificial? Answer me please (write back), if for nothing else, to make it ring true in retrospect. I think I'll try to fall asleep now. With Patsy Cline. While the rain is still clanging and whirring around in the yard like an idiot.

I love you. I'd love to meet you. Can't wait to miss you.
—Fall'n to Pieces

PHILIP, BROTHER, BARTENDER,

This poem is a guitar
which is not in tune
though tuned to itself
& I can't sing anyway
& Julie staked a robin
made of metal
in our winter garden
& it swims a metallic swim
that's a callnote or a racket
& this thing rushes over me now,
outside as sudden & overwhelming
as the stars—which I'm not to write about—
but it's not even a star, that swimming one,
headed up, which is clearly a plane
& I already write of planes, but it's heading straight
towards an actual star. Tomorrow morning, the papers read,
or are read, "132 Passengers Feared Dead
in Plane-Star Collision" & once it's clearly a plane
it's suddenly red occasionally, & no one knows
who's gone, so they study the remains
to see what's human, what's other,
& they do this by sampling
random samples. The dirt
is composite, *i.e.* a compost
of everything around it

& you, friend, & I,
poet, are here
& we're there, swimming,
staked, knowable
only in our din,
our reactive turn,
& I sing the same to you;
our round against rust,
unconvincing though nimble,
anchored, & crude
in delivery
but stubborn, still,
above all, stubborn.

MERLE HAGGARD,

In the end, you looked like my grandfather
in that you looked like you died in 1992.
Such a serious face. You looked so full

of the impending inauguration
of another Clinton. We have not declared war
in my lifetime. It makes me tired.

My eyelids find each other all smiles,
slo-mo explosions. I was promised comfort
& relief, satisfaction or my money back.

My face is apparently still young, if less
& less. I never did heroin, which sounds,
I know, like I listen to every kind of music

but country. I was promised that my post
-modern brand of neurosis would be hailed
as the new confessionalism, *i.e.* "'I want

yr cock in me,' I text to my wife," as measure
of simultaneous male sweetness & of cock.
Models shown with optional features.

At dusk's invitation, slow & with bellysway,
mothers lead young from behind a billboard
to chew beyond its daily shade. There stands

the glass. In the last stubbornness of light
I watch the breeze's flocking trajectory.
The race is on. It is so lonesome I could cry.

It is transient & visible only in its effects,
like any other absence, fondness, or distant
Del Reeves night highway—headlights

lining its curves like harbor lights, like flares.

OUR EMMA, FAIREST WHEN FLEEING,

Don't be discouraged, though we wrote this
in the dressing room of a department store

while moving trucks on Reserve
turned diesel into sky. Your leaving

approaches silent as a shut-in
on a golf cart, name of Bill,

who can't help but mean well.

As you quit this town—a habit
of space—put on your oldest shirt

& ugliest shoes. Listen to Jesus
for a stretch on the FM band.

Keep your sunglasses loaded & ready.

Night, as we know it, is hours away.
When it comes to, we'll drink up wine & sleep

fitfully. When you give up on the Word,
wear a soundtrack angry & earnest

& loud. Try to feel welcome in South Dakota,
Minnesota, wherever. Smile if you have to.

OH, TORPOR. MY DRAWL. MY POOR DRAWN LIGHT,

You're limping through the drapes and reeling feebly forward
toward the best gal and her boyscout belt and cussed mouth.

When sunrise crests, she's a test strip lipping the horizon
& you're gumming cobwebs in the corners and cicada

shells from the screens. The lady next door
has a star tattoo, and is likely to have a name. We just call her

Torpor. My Drawl. She is my neighbor lady & she locks
    herself out,
curls up on the Welcome mat & knocks for hours. The
    painting

of the farm leans south as the couch is fucked against the wall.

The circumference of a kiss is mathematical; congruent
with aghast or a scream. To feel love & shame simultaneously.

Hey, the West, how about naming some more shit after Lewis
    & Clark?

My awful Drawl, how can you be lonesome with a pedal
steel player always with you? I've a story to tell & a breath

made of gin. & then suddenly Victorian; each button mated.
I'm buckled & drawn. Oh, T. The hem of your garment. My hands

frozen as if photographed. We are born again & again

as a storm's boiling nears. With the sound off, we could be
screaming or sighing or yawning. In the winter we dream

of rain. We segue & sequel. We are emphatic
& unreasonable. My drawn light, we will exchange words

& whitened knuckles, blood leaping from my mouth
like song. My buttoned shirt into the kitchen garbage,

another spoiled meal. Love, settle down but listen up:
I may be picking at wasps here, but the sky's really let itself go.

It's tuned to open blue, while across the lake there's fire.
It's colder than it's been & it's been cold.

ANDY WILLIAMS, DEAD AT 84,

Casting from the shoreline's elaborate handshake
seems to yield no take worth taking. The old men recede,
trailing partial prints.

The other shore, the far shore,

is surely settled, certainly a sight
more holy than here. To cross a river, wade
as if of said river. Supine,

unclenched—it's no less than living,
                    a giving-up lighter than drowning.

The smell of bleach has inhabited our fingertips.
I see the fire in my neighbor's eye, through
his blinds, rewinding through the binoculars.

Where'd you get your religion?
Our gated community has our best interests
at heart. Mrs. Tufts has rabbits fleeing
her skirt; those heavily petted are affianced

and look made-up for the bluff.
There are curios. This is a variety
show. Lip-sync with me, stadium-
style, that there's something afloat

in the Branson wind—Mr. Christmas
has to listen—that it's not that easy.

I cannot hope to write you,
flock of cranes—to leave you
folded and stalled in mid-air.

Occasionally we hear of wild bulls
              being tamed and trained as performers.
Occasionally we hear of bears kept
           as domestic pets.

LARRY LEVIS, BIG DEAL,

Just assume these are all ice sculptures—
shapely, uncanny, & doomed.
Each sun, then, a last call
spotlight. Curtsy, slowly, daily.
I will make of your face an adjective.
I want you to believe me
in my hyperbole. I swear
I enjoy comedy, a good time. Well,

Larry, I suppose this is late.
The Old Post gets ready to close
& all the girls go into the bathroom
together & leave together, mysteriously,
thirty seconds later. Their dialogue,
dead stranger, is your eulogy.
I return home, fart into the couch,

observe the outside stumbling in,
endure beer commercials
& the general fading of youth.

The coffee's getting cold, as it does:
each line a last line until the next.

WELL HELL, BIRDIE,

These days refuse to be the days

we predicted. Not enough songs
anymore. With all the lights off,

any view's a panorama. I want to speak

        to my lawyer. I'm so hungry.

Someone says, "Fifteen stitches to the lip."
Somewhere east of town the ash is landing

still. The technician's working on the weather,
entering on crutches, lousy in khaki pants.

Damned considerate of the landscape to provide
        its own aligned wreckage. Look!

More ways to save. For instance, the power
of prayer. Look! at all the things I've shot.

I walk into the bathroom, the backyard,

the basement. Fashioned an antenna.
I took off my jersey, my jewelry,

my face. To accessorize.

You strange off to bed by yourself, lovely
as a treeline on fire. I stayed

on the porch singing God Bless America.

I stayed up all night reading & you
woke just once, saying, "I forgot

I was sleeping," your face taking
on the texture of whatever you sleep against.

Dang it, Birdie Bean,

share your apple with me. Manufactured
tension as evocative of freedom as horses

crossing a river to Lynyrd Skynyrd, as driving

an automobile on a closed road. Do not attempt.

My goal here is to siphon our distances
& burn it all spitting fire, breathing life

as fiction into the dying day. We have over sixty words

for "words"; none for precipitation's smatter

on our air conditioner. As a nation, we are
arresting our elite athletes. We have moments

brought to us by Budweiser. Oh, B, we are relics
of the fluent spectacle; put your hand in my pocket!

KHATY XIONG,

A woman drowned in the Bitterroot
this summer. It is sad, now, & exotic

for these first inches of snow. The high
tomorrow is below the number we have
for nothing. All of our families dying.

If you add hot water to whiskey,
it becomes something of a tea.

I know after winter the weeds
are surface bruises. Khaty,

water freezes first on the skin,
becoming less symmetrical

in its bonding. I wrote this
for you in my kitchen,

but read it as if from
the side of some river.

If you add hot water to the sky—

THAT OTHER GUY FROM THE EAGLES,
DEAD NOT TOO LONG AFTER BOWIE,

I went & got an ugly growth removed, smelled
my own flesh smoking à la electrocautery,
& then drove around thinking about my body.

After listening to the news, which helped remove me
from my body, I took my six pounds of skin for a walk,

looking for something worthwhile. The Art Center
was closed—Monday—so I took myself out

for a double Buffalo Trace at GT. Return

for suture removal in ____ days. Do not
let a thick crust of dried blood or scab

accumulate at the wound site. Now I'm thinking

about how, "You woke up looking for your panties
because you had to get home before your girlfriend

worried," is different than, "You woke up looking
for your panties because it's your turn to take

the dog out." I'm not really a big fan, but I trust you
to recognize the ways the world redefines itself,

breaks up, reunites, breaks up, all that.

ANDREW MARTIN,

We never reminisce about past sadnesses.
We are forward-looking men of imagination
and destiny. I awoke this morning to the blond
head of a teenager coming in through our living
room window. Never too strategic, upon recognition
of the head as a human head, I screamed, "Hey!!"
& the blond head disappeared to be captured
a block away with his haul from neighbors' houses.
I hated him at the time. At the bottom of the list
of helpful events in the context of Julie's profound
anxiety is that blond goddamned head crowning
above our couch. Eight hours later, though, after
most of a beer, I almost regret interrupting
his spree. We're all fashionably bereft of gall
these days. The gusto. On TV, identical women
are making owls & cats out of things you might find
in your pantry, were you the type to have a pantry.
And chives. A friend was choked for being a woman
on the Higgins bridge this last week. The fucker
got beaned with a football & then mobbed. Andrew,
these are all true stories. Andrew, I'm incapable.
The world is getting bigger again. We've been watching
documentaries on cults: charisma, beards. I will travel
to your Virginia. We'll sit under your pregnable windows
& bathe in our twang. There are dead men on the carpets

of our soap operas. Our spangles oscillate so functional
between diamonds & tears.

Stay tuned,
—BJ

ROBERT GOULET, DEAD AT 73,

We are still far from the sea, though
closer now than before and, if it swallows—
as promised—California, closer still

soon. There is a road nearby,
I know; a path onwards towards gas stations
& stoplights & nature preserves & Canada.

We were born in this country & can't help it.
Each of us, in the basement of our blood, is aiming
a firearm at your chiseled chin.

Each road is a spinning black tire & each tire
a fine thin needle, stirring too far into its own
foul bathtub. Our own singing visage is ripe

with anthem. Dear Wrestlemania 6, Lancelot
is top-heavy with moustache, twitching at the radio,
which informs us that love is, in fact, like oxygen.

We are still far from the sea, though.
We will call the thing called love
petty or mighty, lonely or lovely,

depending. We are still far, though
new sentimental tchotchkes
launched from Japan may beach.

Depending on whether we feel ourselves
petty, mighty, etc. we may celebrate, bronze
or burn these Japanese things. This town

they call a city dims in the reckless dusk.
When its failing silhouette is twinned
the town-sized city will disappear, at last.

RACHEL MINDELL,

I don't really smoke, but I smoke with you & I smoked
    tonight,
by myself, so cold my leg jittered like a flag as a plane
    flew over low
& loud. We live by the airport; these things happen.
    Wind is blowing snow

over pre-settled snow. Two seasons later, a fire turns the
    pastoral above it
into a photograph bloated & wavy from a basement
    flood. There's a mother
yelling at her children. There are machines out here to
    dig into the world.

Remember Will, who hit a moose with his motorcycle
    & can now intuit
your honesty? I saw him walking without a shirt,
    shirtless. Rachel, I hope
that you've found something in Arizona what simply
    can't be found here:

an '80s porn saxophone keening while a spadefoot
    buries its eggs
mechanically in the Sonora landscape. I imagine that
    you are on a walk
now, noticing things. I am in the kitchen poisoning
    myself. Get back in town

& the three of us will skin the night & sell its precious
 muscle. The sky itself
has yet to blush. Beyond the horizon lie promises
 of catastrophe, doing their best streetlight pallor,
 viscous light diminishing shyly. A slow, melodramatic
 dusk

will make way for the grayscale. I worry that I'm going
 blind. & I still have some graves to visit. Friends—by
 suicide, murder, aneurysm—populate cemeteries
I've never been to. I don't think you've ever seen me with
 my glasses on. Still,

mainly though, we have these bells hanging from our
 porch light, which doesn't work. Even in this broken
 wind they make no sound but cast a threefold
 shadow
of decreasing definition, & I wanted to write you about
 it, so I did, & this is it.

JAMES TAYLOR, I FORGIVE YOU. GROVELING

in the sweet sawdust, you tell me
you had a dream last night

about cutting off your head.

No, really! When I break a glass
against the shower wall, your spine

gets in line sudden, straight as sports

commentators' teeth. Tonight's
blacknesses align for you.

Where have you been so long
that you don't hear me

longing in the dark? Are you
moving east? Getting married?

Dying? After all, we are surrounded.

There is always such darkness.

Passing your mood-lit windows,
I thought you had a triptych on your wall.

Now I think it was just three turtlenecks hanging

next to each other. I'm on the toilet, feeling
for matches when a car goes by.

Planes circle, vultures crash, then,
of a sudden, the kitchen light lit the crickets'

circuit a-firing. Your turtlenecks would be
worth more, monetarily, if they were
conceptual art. Perhaps you know this

& wear them in defiance. Or perhaps

yours is a model home, all art. Art art art
art art art art. Like that. I found

a bone in the backyard. Apparently
something has died. A car goes by.

There are noises in the night. It's okay.

MORGAN MAURATH,

I decide to continue on despite the suspicious blueness
of it all, the rusted teeth of infected pines,

the crunch of chipmunk
against mountain road.

There are children playing in the water,
doing things with rocks, taking the world

seriously. Night comes to Deerhorn, Oregon,

half an hour later to Sisters,
where fieldlights break
open and blister. As logs retreat to fire, elephant scales

emerge. I missed a call as I drove across some pass.

It's bad. I might as well finish this bottle of wine
I've started. The stars, in their bounty, seem indelicate tonight.

I heard eighty pills & a blade to the inside of both elbows,
but it's your child
by your body on the bed that I can't sleep sober to.

The embers beak—fledglings glowing their hunger,
begging along the wind. Each gust a blinking pulse, unopened.

KIM BELL,

Is it okay if I want to pet your shaved head? I bring no
    laying on of hands,
only tactile compulsion. As I write this, the grease drop on
    my journal breaks free
of the circle I drew around it. Go! Go! Okay, so, obviously,
    this is going to be

an inspirational speech. I imagine an assortment of people
    have captured
healing words & brought them to you, presenting them,
    fully preserved
in your Great Room, melted snow crying from their mail-
    order boots

in front of your raging mantle. Your audience = the storm's
    blackout
in monochrome. I'm married to Jesus. To my country. To
    marriage.
To Julie. Sometimes, she's in the kitchen eating peaches
    from a can;

other times, it's pumpkin. Even your name, Kim Bell, is
    good.
Kim Bell. Kim Bell. I do not want to be, but I am, falling
    asleep, starting
and finishing a bottle of barleywine by myself, in a little
    yellow plastic cup.

The heat here roars like an engine. An airplane engine. Like
  transport & industry.
The air here is heavy with heat, evening turning all the sugar
  dim. Do you try
to forgive the skin its translations? The new breath, sequestered
  in measure,

or in defiance of measure? That's the thing to remember: when I
  finally remove
my glasses, the light doesn't go anywhere, just distinction.
  Forgive the skin its transmissions: a cup with a string to a
  cup with no string. We are ready to surrender.

YOU, OH YOU, TRYING TO LIGHT A FIRECRACKER IN THE SNOW,

I write this for you from Maine with the season & its
    syndromes,
though I'll never go to Maine.   October threatens as
    automatia,

& I write this for you while weeping into my happy hour
    martini
with a turtleneck on & it's dirty, dirty, dirty—
electrifying the dreaming beef in the bafflement of my
    skull.

I'm getting the shakes & chills & the rest: my face
flush & blustering as only a nervous furnace could purport
    to be.
I've been racing our regatta & really just having a marvelous
    summer.
My Common Law faults are best understood in a
    dramatized confession.

This talking cure, loveably ineffectual, is in active revision.
Who longs to be a stranger here,   raise your hands.

RICK SPRINGFIELD, GET OFF MY LAWN.

Get out of my heart. Hang your hair
up & wash your sheets, you monster.

There's a lot to be decided yet
& plenty plenty yet to lose:
your penitent stance, the dogshit
on your boots, your visible ribs.

I scan the Dow ticker tickling my television
& you're less than Sting tonight.

Don't pet my dog. Don't pretend
anymore. All of these streets
are one-way; every last
frumpy sunset a warning.

OH, LIONESS,

You're skin & bones. How long it takes the grass to grow.
Many of the first things you hear are going to be wrong.
When speaking of the assassination, Lawrence Wright

remembered, "Suddenly, it occurred to us that the right
thing to do was to turn on television." Hunt with me.

The man who killed the man who killed the man we'll call
The Sleeping Mountain. Smoking on air. We're overtaking
the hills to watch the casket pass.   Recipe:

preheat the oven to 400 degrees. Place items in baking tray
in oven. Sex against the counter/sink until the smoke
detector goes off. Fan smoke detector with towel,

with pants around ankles. Shake contents of roast pan
& see where things stand. I have no other details.

DONALD J. TRUMP, HYPEROBJECT,

None of the televisions at Eatery A is your head in an aquarium,
for now. In another letter, I just told Philip to go to Greenough
      Park

& watch waxwings feed each other berries like Roman perverts.
Have you seen *Caligula* or *Satyricon?* Those are my two favorite
      movies

about you. First nice day in weeks & my mood suddenly dark as
      the wine shits,
you ruddy fuck. You look like meat piled twixt some shit in an
      Arby's commercial.

First nice day, there's bound to be a car accident.

People smoke more in the West, like it's a casino. Maybe it's the
      forest fires
& the clean air tindering. Of course there are cars trying to
      reach communion

at high speeds, you muppet fuck. It's obvious. It's falling in love
      with the bartender
or drooling on your pillow, dreaming of salt. I'm a truckload of
      firewood.

I can tell a season by its calendar, a smell sometimes by
  its smell,

you perfumed dick. Maybe I'll take up smoking now
  that I'm back
in the Midwest again. Maybe I'll set a tree on fire, you
  effigy

of fragrant repression. Let's keep talking about Romans,
you bloviating rectum. You are raising an army. We'll
  feast on your corpse.

MICHAEL LANDON, DEAD SO LONG,

Ken's Motel's tub won't drain & there's church on television.
When space shuttles disperse into the terrestrial breath,
we send our children outside to catch relics on their tongues.

The day you died, it all conflated. This televisual trap—
fixed but transitive: frontiers, highways, hairlines.

Now my wife naps   & I write this in Ken's bathroom,
where the light won't wake.   Now you're playing fiddle,
driving a truck.   Now you become a step, set

in cement.   Now I drag this indoor chair out
to sit in the sun.   I borrow. It's not mine—none of it.

THOMAS KINKADE, DEAD AT 54,

At 2:55 this morning, unable to sleep,
I came to terms with my mortality
and its insistent coziness. There
was no light. No copyright.
We'll see how long this lasts.

The grass is green, again, Grace
of God, & swarms of Cottage Sparrows,
en masse, are producing their ideal
songs from templates, but desperately,

as if the interior of the structure
might be on fire. What is Spring

if not pastel? A cross if not potential
treasure, a territorial marker?

I try not to notice myself in mirrors.
All this framing, like a first & last
around the middle name. There is the glow

engulfing Placerville, one of every twenty
living rooms, our QVC Bucolia. We
consider the question of audience,

the performance & the product.
We turn on the living room
light & are saturated.

ACKNOWLEDGMENTS

Thanks to the editors of the journals where versions of the following poems first appeared:

"Bea Arthur, Dead at 86," in *Colorado Review.*

"Eric, Supposedly 32," in *Forklift, Ohio.*

"Dearest Alice Notley," in *MiPOesias.*

"Our Emma, Fairest When Fleeing," in *DIAGRAM.*

"Well Hell, Birdie," in *VERSE.*

"Rick Springfield, Get Off My Lawn," in *Tender-loin.*

Thanks mostly to Julie. Thanks also to you few mighty readers who spent time with these specific poems, namely Philip Schaefer, Andrew Martin, Colin Post, Khaty Xiong, Elizabeth Robinson, Patrick Woodcock, Mackenzie Cole, Simon Parkinson, and, mostly, Julie.

Thanks to David, Ed, and Elizabeth for the kind words, to Ander Monson and the NMP folks for their trust and hard work, and I'll thank all the rest of you beautiful people when I get a longer book with more front matter. Thanks mostly to Julie.

BJ SOLOY lives, for now, in Des Moines, Iowa, where he teaches at a community college and works at an animal hospital. He has work in places like *VERSE; Forklift, Ohio; DIAGRAM; BOAAT; Colorado Review; FIELD; Guernica;* and *New American Writing.* Feel free to write him an elegiac letter of celebrity and friendship at <bjsoloy1@gmail.com>.

※

COLOPHON

Text is set in a digital version of Jenson, designed by Robert Slimbach in 1996, and based on the work of punchcutter, printer, and publisher Nicolas Jenson. The titles here are in Futura.

*

NEW MICHIGAN PRESS, based in Tucson, Arizona, prints poetry and prose chapbooks, especially work that transcends traditional genre. Together with DIAGRAM, NMP sponsors a yearly chapbook competition.

DIAGRAM, a journal of text, art, and schematic, is published bimonthly at THEDIAGRAM.COM. Periodic print anthologies are available from the New Michigan Press at NEWMICHIGANPRESS.COM.

CPSIA information can be obtained
at www.ICGtesting.com
Printed in the USA
FSOW01n0124280117
30082FS